- MY STORY -
DERAILED

It's Never Too Late to Get Life Back on Track

by
Tiffany Naiman

Yattira Publishing
Colorado Springs, CO

Unless otherwise noted, all Scripture quotations are taken from the *New King James Version* of the Bible. Copyright © 1979, 1980, 1982 by Thomas Nelson, Inc. Used by permission. All rights reserved.

Scripture quotations marked NLT are taken from *The Holy Bible, New Living Translation*, Copyright© 1196, 2004, 2007 by Tyndale House Foundation. Used by permission. All rights reserved.

The Amplified® Bible (AMPC), Copyright © 1954, 1958, 1962, 1964, 1965, 1987 by The Lockman Foundation. Used by permission. www.Lockman.org

Discover the Keys to Staying Full of God
Copyright © 2008 by Andrew Wommack
Published by Harrison House

Derailed
ISBN 978-1-7326580-8-0
Copyright © 2018 by Tiffany Naiman

Published by Yattira Publishing
Colorado Springs, CO
YattiraLLC@gmail.com

Printed in the United States of America. All rights reserved under International Copyright Law. Contents and/or cover may not be reproduced in whole or in part in any form without the express written consent of the Publisher.

In Loving Memory
of my Dad
Rev. Dale E. Naiman

And
To my Mom
Rev. Connie M. Naiman

I would never have made it this far
without your love and wisdom.
Thank you.

Table of Contents

TABLE OF CONTENTS V
FOREWORD BY CARLIE TERRADEZ VII
INTRODUCTION 1
CHAPTER 1 7
   DIRECTIONS
CHAPTER 2 27
   ADVENTURES
CHAPTER 3 37
   OFF THE RAILS
CHAPTER 4 43
   WRONG TURNS
CHAPTER 5 49
   WAKING UP
CHAPTER 6 57
   COURSE CORRECTION
CHAPTER 7 67
   STEPS OF FAITH
CHAPTER 8 85
   BACK ON TRACK
CHAPTER 9 97
   REDEMPTION
CHAPTER 10 105
   WHAT'S NEXT?

Foreword

Have you ever embarked on a journey with a destination in mind, yet ended up somewhere different? Has life taken you down a path which left you feeling like a failure, out of resources, way off your original course, and with the target you set out to hit now looking like a distant blip on the horizon of unmet dreams? You are not alone and there is hope. In fact, there is a path out of the place called disappointment where so many of us have found ourselves trapped.

Derailed is a story of redemption. It is a journey of the not-so-perfect kind that exposes the heart of the author, along with all of those raw emotions we have all felt, but to which we don't all want to admit! If you need to see a light at the end the of your tunnel—and it not be another train—this book is written for you. It will encourage your soul to carry on and get up one more time, knowing that you are not alone, that failure and course corrections are not fatal, and that God still has good planned for you. No mistake you make can change that! You will win if you don't quit—and this book is the encouragement you need to make it back on track.

– Carlie Terradez
Author & Co-founder of
Terradez Ministries

Introduction

Standing behind the partition, just prior to taking the stage at Charis Bible College, I listened as Daniel Amstutz, the Director of the Worship School, introduced me to the crowd of over 600 students and staff at the 2017 end-of-year talent show. I had a few of those pesky proverbial butterflies flitting about in my stomach, but I wasn't excessively nervous. Although I tend to become rather emotional at the most inopportune times, I wasn't expecting to succumb to emotion; I had sung this particular song many times in the past without any sign of tears.

Daniel began, "Tiffany first attended Charis Bible College back in 2006, but due to circumstances, she was unable to complete her first year. Now, ten years later, she has just completed her first year at Charis Bible College..."

Immediately, my eyes filled with tears, and I desperately battled them: now was not the time to lose it! In that moment, the past decade of my life—full of failure, disappointment, anger at God, and outright rebellion, followed by God's faithful restoration—flashed through my mind in an instant. Marveling at the vastness and impossibility of the journey He had escorted me through, I struggled to keep my tears at bay.

Thankfully, Daniel continued, giving me a short reprieve. "The song Tiffany will be singing is special to her as she sang it regularly in ministry at a home for children years ago. Singing 'Who Am I?' by Casting Crowns: Tiffany Naiman!"

That second part of my intro gave me the seconds I needed to still my quivering lips and chin and fan my eyes to attempt to dry up the tears. As I walked out from behind the partition, onto the stage, I gathered myself by looking up—keeping the pressure of my eyelids off the remaining tears—and exhaled a silent, "Whoo," to continue to pull myself together.

I began strong and reached the chorus, *"Not because of who I am, but because of what You've done..."* I was feeling like I had everything under control. However, as I continued, *"Not because of what I've done, but because of who You are...."* the battle was lost, and I found myself

Introduction

trying to sing through a throat clenching with emotion, chin and lips quivering, with tears pretty much flowing freely. I was moved so deeply as I recognized how, despite my own failures, the Lord had been so incredibly faithful to me.

How embarrassing! I thought. But, I mentally coached myself, *JUST. KEEP. SINGING!* Ultimately, I was able to get it together, and finished strong.

Many said to me later, "You had me crying, too!" I laughed and replied, "Praise God! At least I wasn't the only one!"

Not long after the talent show, I ran into Andrew Wommack, the founder of Andrew Wommack Ministries and Charis Bible College, and (second in significance only to my own dad) my spiritual father, and hero. He mentioned, "You'll have to tell me sometime about coming back to school after ten years!"

I answered in the affirmative, "Of course!" However, wryly, I thought, *Oh, sure, Andrew, with all of your spare time!* Knowing the odds of getting personal time with Andrew were slim-to-none, I figured I would simply write my story down. That way, I could just email him!

So, this all began as a shortened version of the tale, but as I began to reflect on how far I have come, how much I have changed, and how life-changing many of the lessons I have learned truly are, I realized that all these things are meant to be used by God to bring others out of patterns of defeat, as well.

I want all of you to experience the true rest, peace, and freedom I have found! My testimony has expanded into much more than just a short explanation to Andrew of how I came back to Charis after a decade. So, I decided to publish this book for all of you to walk through my journey with me as well.

My life is an open book, so I'll be sharing with you details regarding my frustration, anger at God, and rebellious ways of thinking and behavior. When an individual is raised as a Christian, it is very easy for the enemy to use guilt, shame, and condemnation to shut them up. Well, as most of my friends and family can testify: that is not me!

Although I am exposing publicly some things of which I am not proud, I am no longer bound to them by guilt, shame, condemnation, or regret. God has performed wonderful things in my life, and I have been healed of the wounds that would have held me captive. I know that the negative experiences I have had, the mistakes I've made (the huge vats of stupid that I've jumped into with both feet), and therefore, the lessons I have learned, will only benefit those with whom I share them!

What I have discovered is that the grace of God is not a "license to sin," as some imply in their teaching. Instead, it is **the power of God that enables us** to fulfill His plan for our lives. I am learning how to tap into this supernatural ability from God to say no to ungodliness and instead do the things He desires (Titus 2:12).

As I reveal some of these things in my own life, I want to take you through a journey of relationship, rebellion, reconciliation, redemption, and restoration! Learn from my mistakes and realize that no matter how far afield you have strayed, God can bring you back again. It is never, ever too late!

When I consider everything I have learned, one lesson stands out that is the foundation of everything:

We can never fulfill the perfect destiny that God has planned for us through our own efforts. In everything—the circumstances we want to change, the relationships we wish we had, or wish were different, and even our own behavior and internal struggles—we must learn to stop trying to do the Lord's job and let the Father have His way.

My prayer is that my story will serve to encourage others as a testimony of the supernatural power of God to transform the lives of those whom He never ceases to pursue.

"For **God** is working in you, giving you the ***desire*** and the ***power*** to do what pleases him."
– Philippians 2:13 NLT

Chapter 1

Directions

NEWSFLASH: Things don't always turn out exactly the way we've planned! Reality doesn't always match our expectations. I suppose those statements could come as a surprise to some of *you*, but in *my* life, plans falling apart seemed to be a pretty common occurrence. I'll dive into some of the other details later on, but for now, let's go back to the summer prior to my senior year of college.

It was 2002, and I had just completed my junior year at Oral Roberts University, where I was pursuing a degree in International Relations. That summer, I attended the United States Marine Corps Officer Candidate School, located in Quantico, Virginia.

The *plan* was that after graduating and accepting a commission as an officer in the USMC, I would pursue a potential opportunity to attend the Defense Language Institute, located in Monterey, California, and work in the field of military intelligence. Obviously, the 9/11 terrorist attacks were still recent in the minds of Americans, and I wanted to serve in a way that might make a difference.

However, that's not exactly how it all panned out. My entire junior year I had trained intensely, losing the thirty pounds required of me to qualify. Okay, full disclosure: I trained intensely-*ish*. I could have trained much harder and been way more dedicated in the frequency of my trips to the gym. However, as more of the "band geek" than the "athlete," getting my hind parts moving was... a challenge. If I *had* happened to train more faithfully, perhaps what happened wouldn't have happened. So, what happened?

Well, after I had been at Officer Candidate School for about three weeks, I injured my lower back while training. It was severe enough that, after a week on light duty, they sent me home. I remember sitting in a hallway, waiting to be shipped out, and (if I'm remembering correctly) my Company Commander walked by and asked if I would be back the following summer to complete my training.

"Ma'am! Yes, absolutely, ma'am!" I enthusiastically responded, with exaggerated gusto. Did I want to at the time? Of course! That was a whole year away; I had plenty of time to fix what was broken... didn't I? Well, long story short—I didn't. I never went back; therefore, plans derailed. *POOF!* Gone. No more USMC.

Failure number, what, like 562? But seriously, who's counting? And, yes, I understand what some of you might be thinking: *You got **hurt**! That's not your fault! How could you possibly blame yourself and consider that a true failure?*

Let me explain.

My parents began an intimate relationship with the Lord during the Charismatic renewal in 1971, in a small farming community in western Kansas. In 1983, we moved to Tulsa for my parents to attend RHEMA Bible Training Center. They graduated in 1986, so from the time I was five years old, I was a full-fledged pastor's daughter!

I was born again and baptized in the Holy Spirit as a toddler—before we even moved to Tulsa, I believe. I've had my personal prayer language longer than I can even remember! (For more information on these two things, please get ahold of Terradez Ministries' booklet entitled *Your Life With God*. You can request a free copy by going to Terradez.com/booklet. It explains these topics thoroughly with remarkable simplicity!)

So, I really should have had a handle on the whole how-to-live-a-victorious-Christian-life thing, but I certainly did not!

I "knew" salvation was by grace, through faith, but for some reason, I was in total bondage to "behaving right." I always thought, *God helps those who help themselves.* However, this became a huge problem because I could *never* live up to the standards that I had set for myself.

In reality, I couldn't successfully do very much at all to even come *close* to qualifying as "helping myself," so I was constantly trying and constantly failing. How could I expect God to do His part, when I couldn't manage to do *anything* to fulfill my part of the bargain? This put me in a cycle of depression and failure from which I simply was incapable of escaping, especially without a true understanding of what the grace of God really meant!

Keeping these things in mind, let's go back to Officer Candidate School, for a moment.

We were running what's called a "Fartlek" course. Don't ask me why they call it that, I have no idea. Although, I'm really hoping it's not named after some guy named Fartlek, 'cause that'd just be tragic! (Disclosure: After writing that, I looked it up, so I *do* know what it means, and where it came from, but if I told you, it'd be no fun. I would hate to deprive you of the excitement and adventure of looking it up!)

Directions

Okay, back on course (no pun *really* intended): The Fartlek is an interval training workout of alternating running and calisthenics. We were doing dorsal raises (in short, they are reverse sit-ups for strengthening the lower back), and I felt a bit of a pop, and from that point on, it was pain-city! I'm sure the drill instructors didn't realize that I truly was injured, and that I wasn't just overreacting to the strenuous course. So, I finished, but it wasn't pretty.

The very next day, we strapped on our packs and went on a 5-mile hump. Again, *why* in heaven's name the Marine Corps can't just call them "hikes," or "marches," I'll never know! Regardless, that was my breaking point, and I could not continue.

Now, for a non-believer this would be a non-issue. You get hurt, you go home, no big deal. However, for a 22-year-old Christian girl—raised in a home who believed in divine healing (2 Peter 2:24), *"I can do all things through Christ who strengthens me"* (Philippians 4:13), and speaking to the mountain (Mark 11:24), etc.—this was a *huge* problem! The onus was on *me* to come out of this on top!

Any person of faith would stand their ground, say, "No!" to the pain, command it to go, and *believe God* for healing, knowing that no weapon formed against them will prosper (Isaiah 54:17). Right? Okay, I'd love to actually discuss those doctrines in more detail, but for now, suffice it to say, I didn't do much of that.

Derailed

In fact, I "enjoyed" my light duty. It was *rest*. I didn't have to go crawl around in the mud with the other candidates. I didn't have to run. I didn't have to stand in formation holding my seven-pound rifle. I didn't have to *hurt*, outside of the constant pain in my lower back and hip. It was *easier* to just give up.

See, I thought faith was hard. As I would lay in my bunk during that final week of light duty, I would try to *drum up* the faith that I needed to believe God for healing and to come out of this situation on top: successfully finish my 10-week training of OCS, accept my commission as a Marine Corps First Lieutenant, and sail off into my dreams, with an outstanding testimony of faith as a cherry on top!

Try as I might, I couldn't muster up the gumption to *"...withstand in the evil day, and having done all, to stand"* (Ephesians 6:13). I was tired. My feet hurt. My back hurt. I felt weak. I just wanted to sleep for more than 4 hours. I didn't *want* to stand in faith—I didn't want to *stand* at all! Sitting was good. Laying down? Even better.

So, you see, getting hurt wasn't a good enough reason to avoid considering this a failure. I hadn't failed to become a Marine; I had failed to believe God. I could have been healed—had I had more faith, had I prayed more effectively, had I prayed in tongues more, had I spoken the Word of God more, had I stood up to the pain and the devil's attacks, and pressed through to victory!

No. I had failed as a *Christian*.

Directions

At least, that was my perception.

I don't want to get too side-tracked here, but I know I'm not the only one who has been in a situation like this! I'm certain that many of you have faced a circumstance that was simply beyond your own natural abilities to overcome. So, we become weary, and discouraged, and think, *I just can't fight anymore. I can't stand one more minute!*

Well, that's right! We can't! This is what I didn't understand then, that I understand now: we can't do any of this on our own. That is *exactly* why we needed a *Savior*! It is in these moments of overwhelming pressure, that seem to require superhuman energy to perform, that we must learn to tap into the power of God that is available to us as believers.

However, since I didn't realize that life wasn't all about my own ability, I went home in failure, tail between my legs. I still talked a big game, though! After all, I had told my professors, my friends, and my family of my plans. Internally, I was crushed, depressed, lost. I kept telling everyone that I would be going back after I graduated, but on the inside, I knew that I wouldn't. I didn't have the strength. Well, not the natural strength, anyway, and for the most part that's all I had ever experienced.

Upon returning to school in the fall, I dealt with serious depression and my entire senior year of college was a struggle. My plans had not panned out the way I had anticipated. And that was *really* hard. I was a person who wanted to have a plan and know exactly what was around the corner. I had had my life and future all figured out, so when it fell through, I felt completely adrift.

However, I did manage to graduate, in May of 2003, and moved back to Florida to live with my parents. At first, I just worked temporary jobs through an agency, which was actually nice because I enjoy change! Historically, I would get bored in one place for too long. I also led praise and worship in my parent's church every Sunday morning and Wednesday evening.

During this time, I did learn some awesome spiritual lessons, but I knew there was more for me; I just didn't know what it could be. I considered working with large cats, at a sanctuary, but that didn't feel right.

I knew that I'd always loved missions, and had a gift for learning languages, but I definitely didn't want to be in "the ministry."

Then I heard that teaching English overseas could be pretty lucrative. I thought, *Okay, now we're talking! Travel, adventure, and getting paid for it? I'm in!*

So, in 2004, under a misguided idea that I would pursue a master's degree in teaching English as a second language from my alma mater, I moved back to Tulsa. I enrolled in correspondence courses, which was my first mistake. I did much better in a classroom setting, due to the fact that I am very much a "people person," and I don't do very well with self-motivation. I didn't even complete one course! So, I threw in the towel and withdrew from all of my classes. Yet another failure to add to the list!

I found a job working at a local pet store. I have always loved animals! This job was a challenge, but again, I don't want to go off on a rabbit trail. (Pun absolutely intended!) However, I will say that while working there I adopted two kittens, an iguana, a Burmese python and a western hognose. I was even bitten by a very grumpy, 8-foot Burmese python as well! It wasn't mine, though. And, in her defense, she was *very* sick. Poor thing...

Okay, Tiffany: ***focus!***

Anyway, during this time, between 2004 and 2005, I spent many weekends driving two hours from Tulsa to Pittsburg, Kansas to visit my best friend, Chrissy. She lived with a wonderful married couple, Matt and Sarah, and their small boys.

Now, Matt had been acquainted with Andrew Wommack's teaching for many years and had really gotten Chrissy "on board" as well. Matt was (and still is, of course) a very gifted teacher of the Word, and we would have many discussions about grace. It was really challenging for me, for some reason, to wrap my brain around the fact that God pouring out His goodness on me wasn't dependent upon my actions. It just did not compute!

During this time, I began to listen to Andrew's teaching cassettes in the car while I drove to and from Kansas to visit my friends. I would listen, and then ask Matt questions, and those discussions were the foundation of beginning to understand the truly balanced message of grace and faith. Slowly, I began to see how my faith was part of the equation, but not the only part. God's grace had already provided me with innumerable blessings, and my *believing it* was how I could access them.

In August 2005, I attended my very first Gospel Truth Seminar, hosted by Andrew Wommack Ministries, in Tulsa, OK. I was really excited to finally see Andrew in person and was certainly not disappointed. In addition to being an exceptional teacher of the Word, he was also very personable. I was surprised that he made himself available well before the start of the meetings, and readily greeted and prayed for attendees. He was so graceful about talking to anyone, as long as everything still stayed on schedule! I'd been around many large ministries and knew that his heart for individual people was an uncommon trait. This event is where I first realized his quality as a role model.

I'll never forget the topic he chose for that event: *The Four Keys to Staying Full of God*. How timely! This was exactly the message that my roller-coaster-Christianity existence was starving to hear. Although I had already become habitual regarding listening to Andrew's teaching, from then on, I was truly hooked!

Directions

My friend Chrissy had gotten married earlier that year, and she and her husband, Kevin, decided during that conference that they would move to Colorado Springs to attend Charis Bible College. Chrissy was adamant that I should do the same!

At the time, I had a teeny-tiny glimmer of desire, but I just shook my head and said, "No way!" I wasn't nearly ready to make that kind of step. I mean, it's not that I was particularly happy where I was (I wasn't!), but I didn't want to make such a drastic change. Taking a leap like that is a bit daunting, to say the least.

I also had a very anti-ministry mindset. I had absolutely zero interest in ever going into the five-fold ministry because I had been a pastor's kid for my entire life. I knew one thing about being in full-time ministry: it is **not easy**!

I had seen church splits, back-biting, betrayals—you name it, my family had experienced it. Not that it was all bad! My parents were amazing pastors, there were definitely aspects I enjoyed, and overall, the members of our churches were precious people. I also loved when guest speakers would come, sometimes even staying in our home. As the pastor's daughter, I had close access to these men and women of God, and it was always a blessing!

You would think that the combination of so many people, including my parents, speaking life into me—telling me I could do anything I set my mind to, that God had good plans for me, and that I was loved, blessed, and highly favored—would have set me on a victorious path! But the enemy was subtle in his attacks, and I allowed them to be effective.

So, at first, I was absolutely not interested in Bible College, having zero intention of ever entering the five-fold ministry. However, I *did* want to know more about the Word, about God, and how to grow in intimacy with Him. I knew I wasn't walking in the abundant life God wanted for me, and I also knew that knowing Him would bring the growth in my life that I so greatly wanted to experience.

And I had so many questions!

I remember thinking when I was young, *Jacob was a jerk! He was a liar, and a cheater! Why did God bless him?! Abraham gave his wife away to save his own skin—**twice**! Why was God so good to these people in the Old Testament, even though they weren't very good people?* Or, *Why did God have the Israelites kill everyone in Canaan? Why did they destroy everything, including the kids and animals?* (For really awesome answers to these questions, look up Andrew's teaching on *The True Nature of God*. It will change your life!)

There were so many things I didn't understand, and that was what really motivated my desire to attend Charis Colorado. I wanted to know God more, in the

Directions

hopes that knowing Him more intimately would somehow bring change in my own circumstances and behavior.

I came to the conclusion that I especially wanted to learn through Andrew's ministry. He always just made the Word of God make so much sense! When I heard him teach, he would connect the dots in a way that revealed answers to so many of my questions.

So, it was a week or two after that first conference, around the first or second week of September, when Chrissy and I spoke again over the phone. By that point, after considering all of these things, the teeny-tiny glimmer had bloomed to full-blown desire to attend Charis. I knew in my heart that it was exactly where I needed to be!

It was too late for the September 2005 fall term enrollment, but I had decided to go in November as a winter student. However, it is no surprise that I have an enemy, and he used something that most of us consider to be very ordinary to sabotage what God was doing in my life: television!

I know, that sounds ridiculous, right? Well, even every day, seemingly innocent, things can be harmful when we allow them to get us out of balance. For an early birthday present to myself, I made a *super genius* move and decided to get cable television. Within a very short time I was using that brand new, fancy-schmancy DVR to record nearly 40 hours of television a week! When I woke up, I would watch TV. When I came home from work, I would watch TV. Even though I should have been making preparations to move to Colorado for Bible College, I found myself utterly distracted. The more TV I watched, the less I thought about my future as a student at Charis.

So, over the course of the next few months, the thought of Bible College faded to the far recesses of my mind. I struggled at work (no longer with the pet store, but in a call center) with attendance and basically the job in general. I was absolutely miserable and had a difficult time motivating myself to even go to work! Ultimately, I lost that job because I had missed too many days, and I sought employment at a similar company instead.

Oh, look: another failure.

But God wasn't done with me yet!

Somehow, I picked up Andrew's teaching entitled *Hardness of Heart*. I realized what my problem was: my heart had become so hardened, I couldn't be led by Him effectively. Pumping myself full of natural things, even if they weren't *evil*, brought me to a point of greater sensitivity to natural things, thereby becoming less sensitive to spiritual things. Something had to change.

So, around July 2006, I finally threw out the TV and began to spend more time with God. (Not literally, I just cancelled my cable subscription. No televisions were harmed in the development of this testimony!)

Now, I don't want to give the mistaken impression that I was 24/7 in the Word, getting crazy amazing revelation, and moving into Super-Christian status! Far from it, in fact.

However, I was at least unplugged from the 24/7 focus on the world and natural things. It gave the Holy Spirit room to work in my heart, and to prepare me for the next step, which I never could have imagined at the time.

It was September 28, 2006, when I had another conversation with my dear friend, Chrissy. She and her husband had relocated to Colorado Springs and were doing very well. It was rather late in the evening, and I remember her saying, "Tiffany, I still feel like you are supposed to be out here, going to Charis."

My amazing friend, Chrissy, who has been through it all with me. Faithful friends are priceless!

My mind and body were in complete turmoil, head to toe, inside out! My thoughts were racing, my heart was pounding, and my stomach felt tied up in knots. I just did not see any way to relocate, let alone afford school. And remember, as an animal lover, and having worked for that pet store in 2004, I had my well-loved pets! My gut churned at the thought of rehoming them, not to mention the moving process in general. Sure, two-fifths of them were snakes, but I enjoyed my reptiles very much! (To each her own, right?)

But, after I hung up the phone with my friend that night, even though I desired to move to Colorado, attend Bible College, and just somehow get away from this constant feeling of failure, I was still filled with fear and uncertainty. How would I pay for it? How much would it even cost to move? What would I do with my pets?

Total turmoil.

I told the Lord, "Father, I have no idea what to do! I need a word from You! I need to *know* for sure that this is what You are directing me to do."

So, like many of us do at certain times in our lives, I played "Russian Bible Roulette" and randomly opened the Bible and started to read! I began in 2 Corinthians 1:1 and just kept reading. When I got to chapter eight, verse ten, I felt like a dagger stabbed me in the heart—but in a good way! (It's possible, I promise!)

Directions

"*¹⁰And in this I give advice* (Here it was like I heard my name, '...in this I give advice, **Tiffany**'): *It is to your advantage not only to be doing what you began and were desiring to do a year ago; ¹¹but now you also must complete the doing of it; that as there was a readiness to desire it, so there also may be a completion out of what you have.*"

What you began and were desiring to do a year ago? Well, a year ago—almost exactly, as a matter of fact—I was desiring to attend Charis Colorado! I was just blown away by how specific this Word was for me. It was the first time in my life that I received a RHEMA Word from God—a Word directly from Him to my spirit, that just immediately came alive on the inside of me. I *knew* that He was telling me, "**GO**!" Yet, I still felt the same turmoil, the same indecision, the same fear.

Why?

You know, our emotions can take off without us sometimes, even when we recognize God's voice. How could I *possibly* still feel that way, after the Creator of the universe Himself had spoken to me? Well, I don't know the answer to that question, but that's how it was. So, with the information I had, what would I do?

Going back to my childhood, I remembered my parents always taught me that we have to follow the peace of God in making decisions. Colossians 3:15 says, "*...let the peace of God rule in your hearts...*" Well, the

Amplified Bible translates "rule" as "act as umpire." The Spirit inside of us, giving us peace—or withholding peace—is the One who determines when we are "Safe!" or "Out!" or "That's a foul ball!"

So, how do we do that?

Well, the best way to do this is exactly the way Mom and Dad always taught me! (See? Even in our late twenties, we can still remember and follow the advice of our loving parents!)

They used to say, "When you need to make a decision, just choose one way. Make a choice, even though you haven't acted yet. Write it down. Then, pray on it and sleep on it. If you have peace about that decision, then go ahead. If you continue to feel unsettled, or just that it's somehow not right, then either pray on it a little more, or choose a different option and repeat the process."

It had worked for me in the past, so that's what I did. I opened up my notebook/journal and wrote, "I am moving, in November 2006, to Colorado Springs, CO to attend Charis Bible College. Classes begin November 13th, 2006. I'll be there."

Notice that I didn't write, "Lord, *please* show me whether to go or not." He had already answered me! So, the decision is actually what we do in faith, after hearing the instruction from the Lord, even in the face of uncertainty and/or fear. At first, it's not always a physical action, but simply a mental settling of a matter. I made my choice, and went to sleep, even though I was still freaking out!

When I woke up the next morning, I had *total peace from the inside out*! I'm not exactly sure how to explain it, but the heart pounding anxiety—about the move, my pets, the finances—was totally gone! It had been replaced with a peaceful anticipation of this new thing God was planning.

So, I immediately began preparing to leave. I found homes for my "babies," and started advertising an apartment sale, etc. I was excited! I thought for sure that I'd be out of Tulsa within two weeks.

Yet, although progress was being made, little setbacks kept popping up, pushing back my move date. This frustrated me because I was chomping at the bit to go!

Ultimately, the day finally came when I stuffed everything I possibly could into my 1999 Toyota RAV4, cleaned out my apartment, and struck out in a new direction!

Chapter 2

Adventures

NEWSFLASH: When you're off doing something new (a fresh start, new horizons) the pain of previous failures can somewhat fade into the background in the face of all the excitement. However, when your focus is consistently on yourself, trusting in your own ability (or even lack thereof), you are just making preparations to experience failure all over again. Doesn't the Bible have a verse somewhere that refers to pride coming before a fall... or something (Proverbs 16:18)?

Wow, that's gloomy! Listen, this story is on an uptick, right? Things are looking *good*! That's true. This time of my life was, up until that point, the absolute *best*. I was hearing God more clearly than I ever had before, and for the first time in my life I knew 100% that I was following His plan for my life.

He did so many miraculous things for me that year, and I want to share a few of them with you. Listen, if God can do these things for *me* (and I was as much of a mess as anyone else), just think of the hope *you* can have in Him!

First of all, for a couple of months prior to my relocation to Colorado Springs, my well-loved car had been making a very ugly grinding noise every time I made a right-hand turn. It was loud and scary, but there was truly nothing I could do about it because I simply did not have the extra finances to have it repaired. For the few weeks leading up to my trip, I had a teensy bit of concern regarding its soundness. Yet, when the morning arrived, not really giving it too much thought, I got in my car and drove off on my new adventure!

It's a 10-hour drive from Tulsa, OK to Colorado Springs, CO, but I had so much fun! (I do love a good road trip!) Yet, that little SUV didn't make one little bang, ping, or grinding sound the entire way to Colorado!

That night I settled in on the couch at my friend's home—Kevin and Chrissy again! After the journey, I had it in my heart to open my journal to the page where I made that life-altering decision to move. As I read, my heart gave a little leap: *"I will move to Colorado Springs in November 2006 to attend Charis Bible College."*

That was written on September 28th, and I had wanted to leave as soon as possible, yet I had come up against multiple little obstacles during the month of October that kept me in Tulsa. The night I finally arrived in Colorado Springs was **November 1st**. I had completely forgotten that I had written "November" that night. Amazing!

> 9/28/06 Tonight is Sept. 28th, 2006, and I'm about to make the most important, life-changing descision I've ever made. I am moving, in November 2006, to Colorado Springs, Colorado to attend Charis Bible College. Classes begin Nov. 13th, 2006. I'll be there.

This is a photo of the actual journal entry.

The next morning, my friend Deanna was going to take me to see the school (it was still located in Colorado Springs at that time), and to the mall (where she worked) to apply for a job. She had been staying in Kevin and Chrissy's spare bedroom, and we planned to also begin looking for an apartment that we could share.

We climbed into my car, and I pulled out of the parking spot, turning right. Immediately, the familiar squealing, grinding sound began again! That wasn't a ton of fun, but we drove on down to the Charis building, anyway. We hadn't planned on even going inside, but I used the opportunity to spy out the land and ask around if anyone knew of a mechanic who was associated with the school. They recommended me to a man who was a church member of Charis Christian Center (which would become my home church), so we drove down the street to see him.

I remember that after looking at my car, he looked at me with a very grave expression and said, "Your right hub bearing is completely worn down to the point of being barely held together. That entire wheel could have broken and fallen off your car at any moment!"

Yet, I had driven ten hours the day before, in total peace and safety! God is so good!

I hadn't enrolled yet, but the mechanic still gave me his 15% Charis student discount. However, it still took 50% of my money to fix the car, which left me with only about $200! In my job search, I was unsuccessful because my parents had already booked a flight for me to go home for Thanksgiving. Employers simply didn't want to hire someone who would be leaving for a week very soon. I don't blame them: I wouldn't have hired me either!

My financial needs being met is really a whole other story. In hindsight, as I looked back at that year later on, I had earned $3000 over the entire year, and our rent alone was over $800 per month. I have *no* logical explanation for how that worked, other than God does provide!

Classes did start on November 13th, 2006, and I *was* there! I remember walking in on that first day and being in awe. I loved being there: It was everything I had expected it to be, and more. The instructors all knew the Word but had different gifts and perspectives, and it made for a very rich learning environment.

I forget which month it was, exactly, but Carrie Pickett came to speak to our first-year class. Carrie is a Charis graduate who, at the ripe old age of twenty-one, become the Director of the Russian Charis Bible College extension campus, and served there for 16 years.

She talked about the Charis in Russia and told stories that came out of her experiences there. She was so close to my age; I remember feeling a bit inadequate in comparison, yet I also admired her greatly!

On the surface, it didn't seem that she was saying anything particularly earth-shattering, but I literally cried during the entire class period! Tears rolled down my cheeks, and I really couldn't discern any specific reason why. The only tangible idea was that my heart was deeply moved to hear of the lives being touched by the Gospel in Russia, through Charis, and the ripple effect that those graduates would have as they went out to do the same.

At the end of class, I approached her and tearfully said, "I don't know why I'm crying, but I've been crying through the whole class!"

Carrie hugged me and said, "The Holy Spirit is just doing something in your heart!" That statement brought me a lot of hope, but I didn't understand, and certainly didn't sense anything tangible. All I knew was that if the Holy Spirit was working on me, it was *good news*!

I wanted to give her the world that day. If there had been a million dollars in my pocket—okay, fine, in a briefcase or something—it would have all been hers! Ultimately, I did give Carrie everything I had: a grand total of eight dollars! Only eight dollars to my name—hey, maybe it paid for lunch—but I *so gladly* pulled it out of my pocket and gave it to her. That brought on even more tears because I wished so much that I could give more!

I never forgot that experience, and remember it very clearly to this day, more than a decade later. I'm convinced I will never forget. Now, I have come to understand a little bit more of what was happening, but that is another story for another time!

Very soon after my first encounter with Carrie, I was coming very close to being dismissed from school for non-payment of my tuition. I don't think I had paid much of anything toward my tuition yet, at that point.

As first year students, we were required to perform "service hours," which encompassed everything from volunteering at local ministries to helping on the home front at Charis and AWM. One day—just days prior to being kicked out—I was in the main break room stuffing envelopes, doing my part to help.

The school had developed a new scholarship program, and we were sending out letters regarding the opportunity. I remember as I was stuffing those envelopes, I was praying in the spirit, along with the following *super spiritual* prayer:

"Lord, please don't allow money to get in the way of anyone who is called to attend Charis, 'cause that's just STUPID!"

Hey: short, sweet, to the point. Who says you gotta be all eloquent 'n King James 'n stuff all the time?

As I was praying, one of the instructors came and sat down next to me, and asked, "So, how are your finances going?"

I'm pretty sure the look he got was a mixture of a blank I-have-no-idea-how-to-respond-to-this face, and laughter! So, I told him. It wasn't pretty! If I remember correctly, that Friday would be my last day if I didn't pay my tuition. I honestly only remember him sitting down and asking me that question, but I don't recall how the conversation ended. I just kept on stuffin'!

About 10 minutes later, the Dean of students came out from the back offices and said, "Someone just paid your tuition through April." This was a total of $1242! I jumped up, heart pounding in excitement, and ran through that building praising God! He is truly faithful to His promises!

I just *knew* that my little $8 seed was the catalyst for receiving this harvest!

Things were looking good. I still struggled financially, but my tuition was nearly halfway paid! As a November student, I wouldn't be finished in May, but would continue to attend summer school. I still would have owed more to complete my first year, but that amount guaranteed my admission until around April of 2007.

God had done so many marvelous, miraculous things for me. So, what happened? Isn't this a testimony? Aren't testimonies supposed to begin with a downside, then culminate in a victorious ending? At this point, everything looks rosy! What gives?

Have you ever read the book of Exodus? As you read, you picture all the amazing things God did for the Hebrews: sent plagues to deliver them out of Egypt, not one of them sick or weak, parted the Red Sea so they could cross on dry land, provided manna and quail in the desert, ensured that their clothes and shoes never wore out in 40 years, and much more!

Yet, it was never good enough for them. They continued to gripe and complain! And, as you read, you think to yourself, *Are people really that **stupid**?*

Sigh. Yup. Yes. Indeed.

Chapter 3

Off the Rails

NEWSFLASH: "Off the rails" is an idiom that pretty aptly describes my behavior. I was chugging away, in the place God called me to be, yet I completely jumped off track. Again, I'm not saying this in a condemned or guilt-ridden way. I just marvel at God's unwavering love and faithfulness to His sheep. (Sheep aren't the brightest of animals, by the way.)

Now, I've heard Andrew Wommack say countless times, "How dumb can you be and still breathe?" Thankfully, I am aware this is a rhetorical question and that Andrew doesn't expect an actual response when he asks it. Otherwise, I might feel compelled to offer up my picture as a visual aid!

Okay, I'm not dumb. As a matter of fact, I'm considered to be relatively intelligent. However, most of us have witnessed intelligent minds that do not produce logical thoughts and behaviors. Look around our world today: there are many brilliant people who have been completely deceived into adopting the theory of evolution—regardless of its statistical impossibility—as fact! Whereas I've never fallen for that particularly irritating lie, there were plenty of others that I fell for hook, line, and sinker.

The bottom line is, any time we get off track, those actions can be traced back to a root of pride. As I studied at Charis, I was absolutely growing in my knowledge of the Word and God's true nature. I began to see that negative conditions were *not* the will of God. His desire is that, due to the sacrifice Jesus made for us at the cross, all of His children live *abundant* lives here on Earth.

Yet, I wasn't seeing it come to pass in my own life as quickly as I thought it should. I would study the Word and wouldn't really "feel" any different. I wasn't seeing any progress, not only in my external circumstances, but especially on the inside of myself.

I had been ministering to a couple of teenage girls, who continued to reject making a decision for salvation. It was so hard for me, because they were saying all the right things, they understood what I was teaching them, but they wouldn't say, "Yes," to Jesus! I wasn't seeing healing manifest *instantly*, which I felt was God's perfect will. Another irritation was that I was still struggling financially, even though tuition had been paid.

I wasn't seeing things happen in the way I expected. This impatience caused a lot of frustration.

At the same time, at the age of twenty-seven, not only was I still single, but there also weren't even potential suitors around me that I could see! When I was growing up, I never had many boyfriends. I always felt so much "fluffier" than the popular girls. I wasn't the cheerleader type—I was the band geek. I was smart, loud, and opinionated. A natural-born leader, I tended toward the bossy side of that particular personality set. I could be *obnoxious*, since I didn't really have a very finely pored filter—if I thought it, I said it!

These qualities weren't necessarily the most endearing to young men. However, I now know that none of those qualities were disqualifying factors: I simply needed a revelation of who I was in Christ. My confidence was based entirely upon what others said or thought of me; therefore, I was very insecure.

Basically, after facing years of rejection from guys, I felt that God had forgotten all about me: He had failed me! I had begun to feel extremely strong stirrings of resentment in my heart toward God regarding my single status, in addition to the other frustrations I had allowed to take root.

As these roots grew deeper, while in that place of vulnerability, I travelled to visit a couple—who are more like my brother and sister, rather than mere friends—in Tulsa, OK for spring break. They played a computer video game that I really enjoyed. It certainly provided an escape from the frustrations that I had been struggling with!

Subsequently, I purchased a laptop computer, and this game that was a harmless hobby for my friends became an obsession for me. Upon returning to Colorado, I spent an increasing amount of time playing that game, through which I met a guy and very quickly became utterly infatuated.

There I was, 27 years old, and I thought for sure God would have sent me a husband by that point! This guy that I had met online—playing a video game of all things—was kind, compassionate, considerate, honest to a fault, and had more integrity than many *Christian* men that I had met! It simply was *not fair* that God would tell me I couldn't be with this guy, just because he didn't believe in Jesus as his Savior!

So, with this new carnal distraction of a video game (simply a repeat performance of what had happened in my addiction to cable television), as well as a new relationship, I was transitioning from merely impatience and frustration to downright anger. In my pride, I decided that God just didn't know what He was doing. This may not have been a conscious thought, but it was a very effective deception, nonetheless.

In complete rebellion against the voice of God, the encouragement from my friends and parents, and what I had already been taught from the Word, I allowed myself to be drawn away by my own desires (James 1:14). As I continued in my addiction, not only to the video game itself, but also to this new relationship, I began to skip class, skip work, and completely withdraw from my friends.

It didn't take long before I was out of money, and out of hope that I could stay. I used to tell people that the reason I left Charis was simply because I ran out of money. Years ago, I finally admitted the truth—I didn't run out of money. I ran out of focus. My eyes were no longer on Jesus (I'm not sure they ever truly *were* 100% on Him), but on my self-self-self!

Self-focus—navel-gazing, *pride*—never results in freedom. Whether we are thinking too highly of ourselves or beating ourselves up, focusing on self simply drags us further down, and more securely entrenched, in the very quicksand we are so desperate to escape.

Failure number...well, darn it, I lost count.

Chapter 4

Wrong Turns

NEWSFLASH: Once you make a couple wrong turns, it is easy to get hopelessly lost. After leaving Colorado, that's a bit how I felt: completely turned around and uncertain of which way was up.

At first, I moved to Texas and lived with another one of my best friends, Amy, and her husband, Jamie. Amy and I had lofty plans to open a business there, but as so many times before, it didn't work out as we'd planned. Three months later, specifically because my social withdrawal and addiction had caused me to alienate the vast majority of my friends, including first

Derailed

Chrissy, and then most recently Amy—two of my *best* friends—I moved back to Florida to live with my parents.

To me, I think this was perhaps the darkest moment of my life. Totally alone, no friends to understand, parents disapproving of this relationship to which I was still clinging (although I had broken up with him *twice*), working 14 hours a week as a barista in a coffee shop, totally broke and in debt up to my eyeballs—it was *not good*.

Yet, even though *I* was completely unfaithful, *God* was still faithful to me!

I became frustrated with my job because not only was I only working around 14 hours per week, but my coworkers also weren't "doing things right." I'm a stickler for the rules, for policy, and *especially* for recipes! So, when I saw them not doing things the way they should (to absolute perfection, of course), I would try to influence them, but as I had zero authority, of course they wouldn't listen. Wow. I was such a pain!

So (me being the natural leader that I am), I got tired of it and decided I wanted to be the boss! Through a series of divine appointments, and supernatural favor, I was hired by a restaurant company as a Manager Trainee and started work on my 28th birthday: October 14th, 2008. To make a long story short, (folks, you have just witnessed a miracle!) within 15 months I was promoted to District Manager.

At the time of my promotion, in January of 2010, I was transferred from Lake City, Florida to Dothan, Alabama. This was the point at which my long-distance boyfriend moved, and we began living together. I mean, what's the point in paying *two* rents, when you can live in the same apartment? That's just *frugal*, right? (I hear Andrew Wommack's voice again, "How dumb can you be and still breathe?")

After a year in Alabama, the District Manager position in Lake City opened again, and I decided that, due to my father's poor health, I would transfer back there to be close to my parents. My boyfriend moved with me, and soon I purchased my first home.

By this point, my family had resigned themselves to the fact that my boyfriend would be around for the long-haul. And, in fact, they really liked him! As I said, he is a *really* good guy. Anytime my mom needed help, he made himself available. He actually helped out more than I did! He had a great relationship with my family, and I had a close relationship with his family, as well.

However, during the following months, into 2013, our relationship went downhill pretty quickly. We didn't fight—I honestly kinda felt that he never *cared* enough to fight! However, it was actually just more that he didn't like conflict and confrontation any more than I did; contrary to my normal opinionated personality, I chose not to engage... usually. Although we didn't fight, we didn't communicate at all, either. In fact, many times he would walk through a room without even acknowledging my existence. I'm not sure if I can adequately express the physical pain my chest would feel every single time it happened. It broke my heart!

Now, I suppose it would be helpful to understand that growing up I never felt "accepted." I was always a little different, and regularly felt like an outcast. I mentioned earlier that I hadn't had many boyfriends, but there had certainly been a string of "unrequited love" situations. So, here I was, rejected again, and again, and again—and in my own home!

In addition, I was spiritually not in a good place. In fact, I think it was during this time that I realized that, although I had been born again and baptized in the Holy Spirit as a toddler, I hadn't prayed in tongues for probably two years! What a realization. Man, was I a mess!

Yet, every time Andrew came out with a new book, I ordered it! I had become a World Outreach and Foundation Builders partner in 2008 and gave pretty faithfully. Practically from the time I drove away from Colorado, I dreamed of returning someday. In fact, I would regularly scan the job opportunities at Andrew Wommack Ministries, hoping something would fit. I knew that's where God had called me, but I had messed it all up. So, I was still listening to Andrew's teaching on a regular basis, but I didn't have any kind of true fellowship with God.

Honestly, I was afraid to talk to the Lord. I knew the Word taught us not to be unequally yoked together with unbelievers, so I was afraid that the Lord would ask me to do something that I would feel truly incapable of doing. So, I just didn't ask, and certainly wasn't listening! Even though I felt rejected by my boyfriend, I still was bound to our relationship. My heart was wrapped up in it, connected to him in the realm of my soul, and that emotional tether (among other things) was keeping me from fully trusting God with my life.

Although our relationship was obviously—to both of us, although we didn't talk about it—on a downhill slope, in March of 2013 I discovered that I was pregnant. I'm not sure how to describe my reaction in writing, but basically it was a softly exhaled, "Huh." Interesting. I took another test. Positive again. "Huh."

I was actually running late to go to my parent's house to try on a dress that needed altering. So, directly after discovering I was pregnant, I had to tell my mom. Well, I suppose I didn't *have* to: I was thirty-two years old! But, although I hadn't been the best of daughters, my mom was always my biggest cheerleader. Who else would I want to be in on this thing from the very start?

I was terrified to tell her, but I fessed up, and she didn't freak out... much. Although getting pregnant outside of a marriage relationship wasn't ideal, after the initial shock, I think she was just excited I wasn't going to die of old age without procreating!

Derailed

Later on that day, my boyfriend got home from work and sat down in the recliner to eat his dinner. I looked at him from my seat on the couch and told him, "I'm pregnant." His response was the echo of my own, "Huh." A similar little grunt.

Well, what now? Here I am, a pastor's daughter, who at the age of thirty-two is now pregnant out of wedlock! Could I possibly have taken the definition of failure to a higher level? Or, would that be a *lower* level? Anyway, I had already failed in such a huge way in so many areas. Let me count the ways...

Oh, wait. I remember, now. I've lost count.

Chapter 5

Waking Up

NEWSFLASH: When you are deeply asleep, sometimes you need a bucket of cold water to the face to get you moving! Thank the Lord, that wasn't exactly the wake-up call I got. It was a lot less... wet.

However, when I saw that positive pregnancy test result, I had a "prodigal son" moment. The Word says that the prodigal son *"came to himself..."* Well, that is exactly what happened. I had a moment of clarity, when I realized, *I do not want to raise my child to think that the way I am living is okay. This is not okay!*

Now, I didn't even mean living with someone outside of marriage. The part that was absolutely unacceptable was that I was not living the abundant life—God's will, plans, purposes, wholeness, and prosperity—that I knew He wanted for me. I did not want my child to think that this unfulfilled, aimless existence was normal. I determined that somehow, some way, God was going to get me to the place where I was actually living out what I believed in my heart to be the truth!

However, in all honesty, I didn't see any possible way to get to a place where we could live that life. But, at some point I heard Andrew Wommack say, "God is your GPS—your God Positioning System. When you take a wrong turn, He just says, 'Rerouting.'" So, I didn't know how, but I had hope that God would *somehow* reroute me.

When I was around 8 weeks pregnant, in May of 2013, I flew out to Colorado to visit my friends, Kevin and Chrissy. The neat thing is that Chrissy had gotten pregnant about 2 weeks after I did! So, we were really excited to spend some time together.

In catching up, I expressed to Chrissy that I didn't see any way that I could finish Charis. We discussed the option of my taking correspondence classes, or attending one of the extension schools, in Jacksonville or Tallahassee. But I worked 50+ hours per week for my company: with a 6 days on, 2 days off rotation. And during the 6 days, I was on call 24 hours a day, so I didn't really see how I could possibly attend school.

Well, I looked up information online, and somewhere I discovered that the Jacksonville Charis campus had classes one night per week at an extension, held in a Lake City church! What? I didn't even know there *was* a church in my area that was affiliated with Andrew Wommack Ministries or Charis Bible College! Maybe this was a *little bit* possible?

Now, Kevin had been working for Andrew's television department, and one day he said, "Hey, Andrew is filming his program tomorrow. Would you like to sit in on an episode?"

Are you kidding me? It took about a split second for me to say, "YES! I'd love to!"

Like I mentioned earlier, I had been a Foundation Builders partner for years and was super passionate about seeing the new Woodland Park campus. Unfortunately, it was under heavy construction at the time, and the property was closed. So, I couldn't go there, *but* I could see a taping of Andrew's program?! I was in!

They let me sit *in the same room*, a little off to the side, next to Andrew's make-up girl. I have searched for the episode that I witnessed, but have never been able to find it, so I'm not even sure what the topic was! However, I will never forget that Andrew said something about even if someone was in an adulterous relationship, God still heard them, and they could still be blessed! This was exactly what I needed to hear to build my faith that God

Derailed

could redeem what had been lost. I began to cry, but at the same time was trying to stifle my tears, thinking, *Be quiet! No sniffles, ya big baby—they're recording!!*

After the program, my friend, Chrissy, and I had a moment to speak with Andrew. I briefly told him that "six years ago" I had attended Charis, but that I hadn't finished my first year, and gave him just a small bit of my story.

He looked at me and said, "Well, you need to finish what you started!"

My response was a bit sheepish, "Yes, sir, I know..."

So, we told him what we had found out about the extension program in Lake City, and he said, "Well, God's just taking away any excuses you might have!"

Andrew Wommack and I
May 6, 2013

"Yes, sir..." I mean, when Andrew Wommack tells you that God is removing every excuse, and that you need to finish what you started: you tend to listen!

I was *so blessed*. I got to sit in on his program, speak with him, and he prayed for me and both of our babies. He also gave me even more wisdom. What an amazing moment!

When I returned home, I knew I couldn't attend weekly church services, due to my work schedule, but I went on most open Sundays (at least for a year or so). Grace City Church (now City Church) was exactly the church family I needed. Here I was, pregnant out of wedlock, but no one ever batted an eye over it! They just accepted me, made me feel welcome and loved, and helped my hope to grow.

So, as I investigated the extension program, I found that it was one night per week for 3 hours. It would take 3 years to complete the first-year curriculum. But I was in! I knew it was God!

I attended classes for a while, but ultimately, I got too pregnant, and my work schedule was too intense, so I couldn't continue. I could count that yet another failure, but it's okay: God had plans!

On December 9th, 2013, my beautiful daughter was born! I had to be induced (she was two weeks late) and ended up with a sort-of emergency C-section (she was stuck). Parenthood: isn't that a whole other story as well? She was beautiful, healthy, and strong, and I was *so glad she was finally out*!!

Derailed

Let's move on.

I went back to work when Ziva was 7.5 weeks old, and it was *hard*!!! My job was very demanding, both physically and mentally. And, no matter what my intentions, I was super grumpy. A LOT! My poor employees got the brunt of it when I was frustrated. That frustrated *me*, so it just escalated my frustration.

But it paid the bills, and I knew I was blessed to have that job—so blessed! I was making roughly $65k-$80k per year! However, since I was deeply in debt, I thought, *If I move to Colorado to attend Bible College again, where/how could I ever make the kind of money I would need?* This is *not* an attitude of faith, by the way! Some people might say, "Well, no, that's just being *realistic* and using *wisdom*."

Well, I'm just gonna throw this one out there, although I don't have time to really flesh it out: Sometimes God's wisdom doesn't look like man's wisdom. In fact, it can look *completely opposite*!

Meanwhile, my boyfriend and I, whereas there wasn't really any romance, got along really well. He is a great father to her! I was very strongly connected to him, and he was still my best friend, so I simply couldn't imagine ever leaving him, or asking him to leave. We had been "together" since 2007 and lived together for years. I certainly loved him, although it was not the way to love God would have had for me. I was emotionally bound to him so tightly—how could I ever move away?

Also, my dad's health was declining rapidly. It had started years ago with a prostate cancer diagnosis. What followed were complications from surgery, which led to the aggravation of a neurological disorder. The treatment for that was steroids, which broke his body down, and he developed diabetes, which led to circulation issues, where he ultimately had to have both legs amputated below the knee.

So, Dad was in an assisted living facility, and Mom had downsized. It was somewhat of a heartbreak that she had to sell the beautiful house she had designed from the foundation up, and in the process losing money on the deal due to the market having taken a huge dive. She purchased a smaller house and fixed it up to her specifications. It was around that time, in 2014, that upon moving she said, "I am **never** moving again!" She was *done*.

I just knew in my heart that I was going to be in Florida until my parents died!

I understand that sounds horrible! But I knew my brother couldn't step up to help: it was on my shoulders to be there for my mom and dad. Who else would take care of them? How could I move away, leave them alone, and take away their granddaughter? I just couldn't.

I was stuck.

This is the condition I found myself in by the time my daughter was nearly a year-and-a-half old: in emotional bondage to her dad; stuck in Florida, because there was no way my parents would ever move; enslaved by a job where I was miserable but making decent money; and to top it all off—AFRAID TO EVEN TALK TO GOD! Wow, what a disaster!

However, I still kept hearing Andrew Wommack say, "God is your GPS, your God Positioning System. When you make a wrong turn, He just says 'Rerouting.'"

I was in such a deep depression, with seemingly no way out. I felt like a complete and utter failure, not only in the large decisions I had made, but in every single day little things as well. Parenting, keeping the house clean (rather, the *not* keeping the house clean—my boyfriend did most of that), doing my job efficiently without being a total jerk-boss (that was rare)—the list goes on and on.

I didn't know how God could possibly get me back to the last thing He told me to do, but the idea of Him just saying, "rerouting," or "recalculating," gave me hope that one day He could!

Chapter 6

Course Correction

NEWSFLASH: When you receive a course correction, it can come with some initial discomfort, mostly due to the realization that so much time was "wasted" with aimless wandering. However, for the most part, going back in the right direction is a relief because you know that you're finally back on track!

Andrew was coming to Orlando! My mom had attended, and enjoyed, a Jacksonville Gospel Truth Rally with me, so she agreed to attend the April 2015 Orlando Gospel Truth Seminar with me as well. Leaving the baby with her dad, we drove the 2.5 hours to Orlando.

It was amazing! Andrew taught on pride, *cough* I mean, *Humility: The Path to More Grace*. (It was on pride, the way I heard it, but that's not the title of the teaching!) It was so good, because I knew God was telling me to just stop doing things my way, and to simply agree with Him. But I was so lost at this point, I had no idea how to do that!

The very last night, I approached one of the prayer ministers. Ready to unload the extremely drawn-out drama of my life to him, I began by saying, "I've gotten myself into a really bad situation. I'm living with my boyfriend, we have a one-and-a-half-year-old daughter, and—" At that point, he kindly interrupted what was gearing up to be a very long recounting of my entire pitiful tale of woe!

He said, "I'm sorry, I really don't mean to interrupt, but I feel the Lord saying very strongly to tell you to focus on your relationship with Him (God) and let him (my boyfriend) make his own choices."

At that, I began to weep, "That's what I need! I need him (my boyfriend) to make the choices because I just can't!" At that moment, I was thinking that God was giving me a way out of making those decisions that were causing such emotional turmoil. However, that's not exactly what was happening.

But, after that man prayed for me, I felt immediately like a huge weight had lifted off my shoulders. I almost questioned it: God wanted me to focus on my relationship with Him? He wasn't angry with me! He wasn't asking me to make any big decisions, or "do" anything special, different, or big. He just wanted me. I felt, for the first time in years, like I could breathe!

Now, you'd think after 13 years or so of hearing Andrew Wommack say, "God's not mad at you; He's not even in a bad mood," I woulda figured that out by this point, but I guess I'm just thick!

I began doing exactly what the prayer minister had encouraged me to do: I focused on God! Now, please don't misunderstand me: I did not turn into a disciplined, nose in my Bible, hearing God's voice clearly every day, walking on cloud nine all the time, success! Far from it! I was still a big mess!

I'd still go days, sometimes weeks, without cracking open my Bible. I wasn't praying significantly more often than I had been. Oh my, I was still very depressed! But something was different. I could talk to God without that cloud of guilt and condemnation hanging over my head! The wall that had been keeping me from His presence, that had blocked the lines of communication, had been broken down. So, over the course of the following months, I became more and more sensitive to His voice.

I had told myself for years that I couldn't hear God's voice, that I didn't understand it when people talked about "relationship" with God, because I didn't really feel I had experienced that relationship with any real consistency. But, during this time, one day I was reading in John 10 where Jesus said, "Hey, you're my sheep. That means that you hear my voice, and not only that, you follow me" (John 10:27)! I thought, *Wait a minute. I'm one of His sheep. And Jesus said right here, written in red, that I do hear Him, and that I do follow Him!*

I decided to stop confessing to myself that I couldn't hear God's voice. I knew I was one of His sheep, and since I also believed that the Word of God is true, and that Jesus could not lie, I knew this must be true! I *did* hear His voice, and I *did* follow Him!

Not long after that I realized that I was hearing Him! He also began to remind me of times in the past where I had heard Him but hadn't realized it was Him at the time. In fact, those times were so natural, that I thought it was just me, or coincidence that I had learned something, etc. Nope. He is always speaking. Sometimes we hear Him, and since we are expecting God to speak in some booming, King James Version sounding voice, we miss the realization that it is Him!

Slowly, but surely, God was working on me. It was months later when I realized that one of my obstacles had been taken care of, without me even noticing it: my heart had healed!

I looked at my boyfriend, and I wasn't "in love" with him anymore. Did I still love him? Absolutely—in fact,

I still love him, to this day. I am so blessed because we have an excellent friendship and co-parent very well together, praise God!

Remember how I said that he used to walk through a room, and not even acknowledge my presence? Honestly, I think if it hadn't been for me, we never would have spoken at all! Yet, there came a day when I knew that the Healer of the broken-hearted, the Restorer of souls, had totally and completely healed my heart and restored my soul!

One day he walked by and ignored me, yet again. And I was fine! It used to devastate my heart, but this time I was completely unaffected. I knew I was free!

Did I still have little twinges occasionally? Sure! But they didn't last. I brushed them off, and the hurt didn't penetrate. So, that was one obstacle to returning to Colorado gone. As I had opened myself up to God, through relationship that was free from guilt and condemnation, He was able to walk in that door and heal my heart. Praise the Lord!

Now, perhaps my heart was healed, and I could at least fathom taking my daughter to Colorado—although, I had anxiety about how her dad would react. However, I still had my parents and my job to consider!

I had mentioned to my mother at some point that, of course, someday I'd love to move back to Colorado to finish

Charis. But, in my heart I knew there was just no way I would leave them and take Ziva. She was their world! Even Dad lived for her visits to him in the assisted living facility.

So, you can imagine my surprise, when around December 2015, one day my mother looked at me and casually said, "You know, if you decide to move back to Colorado for Bible College again, why don't we just all go?"

I'm not sure how I looked at her, or even if I did, but I don't hide my feelings well, so I wonder if it was expressive of what I was thinking: *I'm sorry, what just happened?* I was shocked that she would *ever* consider moving to Colorado! But God had been speaking to her and preparing her heart! (I finally had the nerve to actually ask a year later, but right then I wasn't gonna push it—I just said, "Okay!" Apparently, God had been speaking to her about it, and convincing her it was the best move for us all.)

Well, my three big obstacles were coming down, one-by-one! *"Another one bites the dust!"* Still... With my financial situation, it just didn't seem possible for me to return to Charis. I had a lot of faith, right? At least, at this point, the hope was rising! But I still had my income to think about. I was struggling to pay bills with $70k, how could I manage moving?

On January 3, 2016, I was reading Psalms 107:7, *"And He led them forth by the right way, That they might go to a city for a dwelling place."*

Then I read Psalms 107:30:

"Then they are glad because they are quiet; So He guides them to their desired haven."

These verses hit me right away, and I grabbed them for myself! I spoke over myself that I was being led by the right way, and that I would go to dwell in Colorado Springs, which was my desired haven!

Interestingly enough, there was another verse that really stood out to me that day:

"He will not be afraid of evil tidings; His heart is steadfast, trusting in the Lord." – Psalms 112:7

I thought, *Well, now, that one isn't really blessin' my socks off, but I suppose that's a good one to have in the arsenal?* It had jumped out at me so strongly, I made sure it was readily available to me, just like the others.

Meanwhile, that well-paying job was really stressing me out! My pay had dropped because my restaurants weren't performing as well in the areas on which our corporate office was focused. It wasn't just the pay: obviously it was my performance.

I was having trouble staffing my stores, teaching a relatively new manager how to do everything, and dealing with employee drama. When people would call in, at times resulting in insufficient staff to cover the shifts, I

Derailed

would have to work extra hours. I was getting worn out under all the pressure. But, again, the money. I needed it!

Oh, Abba, you have such a sense of humor!

Not even a week after I had read those verses, my bosses asked me to meet them in a nearby restaurant. That was not a good sign! Long story short—I got demoted. No longer a district manager, I would take over my old restaurant again as the unit manager. Now, granted, I was stressed out, so a tiny part of me was relieved! However, my salary was cut by roughly 50%, from around $70k per year to about $35-$40k per year (the $40k if I was lucky)!

They were very sweet about the whole thing and gave me a couple mercy days off to get myself together. Honestly, my feelings were hurt! Here it was: yet another failure to add to my list! So, I began to think about that salary. Man, losing all of that money was gonna hurt!

Yet, since it was so fresh in my heart, Psalm 112:7 popped up in my heart: *"He will not be afraid of evil tidings; His heart is steadfast, trusting in the Lord."*

Okay, Lord, I prayed. *I'm not gonna be afraid about the money. I am relieved to have some of that pressure off me now. And I'm going to trust You!*

Then, with tears rolling down my face, still feeling a bit pitiful and sorry for myself, rejected and hurt, I heard very clearly that still small voice I'd just recently become accustomed to hearing.

And I swear I could hear a hint of **laughter** in His voice!

"So. What's your excuse *now*, kid?"

I had to laugh, even through my tears. The last chain holding me to Florida had broken, the final wall keeping me back had fallen down! So, I responded the only way I could: "Well, I guess I don't have one anymore!"

The bottom line was this: If I wasn't going to be able to pay my bills in Florida, then I may as well not be able to pay my bills in Colorado! At least there I could believe God, because I would have the security in knowing that I was in His perfect will for my life!

Was it a cut and dried choice at that point? No way! I was freaking out! But, yet again, God still had a plan. And, in fact, He immediately prompted me on that first next step.

Chapter 7

Steps of Faith

NEWSFLASH: Sometimes the steps of faith in which the Holy Spirit leads you make a lot of sense, and sometimes they don't. Regardless: listen!

Right away, after my demotion, I began to tithe to the church I had attended in Colorado Springs back in 2006—Charis Christian Center. Not only had Lawson Perdue been one of my favorite teachers, but he had also been my pastor! So, I felt that I should claim CCC as my "home church" and began to give my tithe to them every payday. I *had* been giving my tithe—mostly, but not always—to Andrew Wommack Ministries, because I hadn't been attending my home church in Lake City very regularly at all. But, at that point, my heart redirected, in faith, to Charis Christian Center, as I claimed it as mine.

In February 2016, Andrew came back to Orlando, and so did I!

Since I had been demoted, I didn't really have the money to go to another Gospel Truth Seminar. My mom couldn't go, so I *certainly* couldn't afford to go by myself! What to do? I *really* wanted (and needed) to go, but how?

Years prior, I had gone to high school with, and taught swimming lessons to, a couple of beautiful girls. They were both a year or two younger than I was. Now, when I had first attended the Charis extension school classes, I had reconnected with their mom, Gwen. What a small world it is when God is involved with divine connections!

So, I asked my friend Gwen if she was going to the meeting, and if so, if I could tag along. At the time, she thought her hotel room would be full, but *since God handles these things*, of course it turned out that there was room for me! So, we went together, with a couple other ladies. Gwen's older daughter, Ariel, even met us there. We had *so much fun*! I loved being with them.

At every Gospel Truth Seminar with Andrew Wommack Ministries, there is always a reception for ministry partners. Now, do you remember that I had wanted for years to work for the ministry? Well, I felt the Lord impress me to tell Andrew, "One day I will work for your ministry."

I did *not* want to do that! I thought Andrew would think I was a crazy, flakey, loopy, groupie, stalker-person! Not exactly the impression I would want to leave with my role model! (Keep in mind, it had been nearly three years since I had met with him in Colorado. I knew he wouldn't remember me.)

But, on the other hand, I knew what God was doing: It wasn't that *Andrew* needed to hear me say that I'd work for him someday—he doesn't do the hiring! It was *me* who needed to speak and

Andrew and I, after I told him I would work for him one day. February 12, 2016

hear that declaration, in faith, requiring boldness in a situation that caused a slight bit of discomfort.

So, I did it! Did I feel like a complete idiot? Of course! But Andrew gracefully shook my hand, nodded his head, and said, "Amen." He may have added a "Praise the Lord," as well, but I was too embarrassed to retain it, if he did.

I walked away, feeling like a total dunce. Apparently, my faith wasn't too strong, and I was having a lot of self-doubt! It's interesting that even when we know we are doing exactly what the Lord told us to do, we can still have uncertainty. That is exactly how I felt as I walked into the "sanctuary" and saw Carlie Terradez at the back of the main conference room.

In case you don't know who Carlie is, I will just say that she is *incredible*. She and her husband, Ashley, are from England, and their daughter, Hannah, was miraculously healed at the age of three from a terminal condition at one of Andrew's conferences there. (Watch their *amazing* testimony on their website at Terradez.com.) After graduating from Charis Bible College in England, they immigrated to the U.S.A., and worked for Andrew for many years.

In fact, months prior to this conference, during my search for a position at the ministry, I had applied for a job that, unbeknownst to me at the time, was actually in Ashley's department. He had kindly called me to let me know that I hadn't gotten the job, which I thought was very considerate! In the course of that conversation, he encouraged me and prayed with me. Even after that day, he would respond to emails if I had questions or needed prayer. In short, Ashley had been an indescribable help to me at a time in which I very much needed it!

So, here was Carlie, who didn't know me from Adam, and I approached her. I told her, "I really want to work for the ministry someday, but can you pray with me that if this desire is not of God that He will take it away?" At this point I became *super* pitiful, and tears joined the pity party, "...Because I don't want to want this for years and have it never happen!"

Carlie looked me square in the eye, from her five-foot-nothing frame, and boldly said (in her most adorable British accent), "No, I'm not gonna pray for you for that! You're being double-minded!" I tell you what, the tears dried up pretty quickly, at that! She continued, "What do you want?!"

Wide-eyed, and a little taken aback, I said, "I want to work for AWM!"

She said, "Well, there you go!"

Let me tell you something: I got it! I understood!

So, I confidently nodded my head, "You're right! I *am* being double-minded! You don't need to pray for me, thank you very much!" And I walked away.

I wanted to work for Andrew Wommack Ministries. The Word says that as we delight in the Lord, He gives us the desires of our hearts (Psalm 37:4)!

My heart to work for the ministry, and to return to Charis, were God's desires planted inside of me! Why would I pray for Him to take away the desires He had for me? No way! Right then, I understood, and I determined that what I told Andrew was true. I *would* work for his ministry one day!

At that time, I didn't see a way for us to move: it did not seem possible! I had a home I needed to sell, I was in debt up to my eyeballs and barely keeping ahead of minimum payments, and moving is expensive! Both my mom and I would have to sell our homes and relocate my dad from his assisted living facility in Florida to one in Colorado.

Where would we live? Would I have childcare? Where would I work? How could I possibly pay my tuition, rent, childcare, etc.?

It looked impossible, and downright irresponsible to do what I was planning.

However, I somehow knew that it was *finally* the time for me to do what I had been desiring to do for years: get back on the path the Father had set me on so many years ago. It was now or never, and never was absolutely *not* an option!

Over the next few months my mom and I both listed our homes, and I began to tell my employers and employees that I would be moving to Colorado to attend Bible College. I told my bosses that as soon as my house sold, I would let them know. Worldly wisdom might say, "Don't tell your bosses what you're planning! They might get rid of you too soon. Or, what if they hire your replacement, and it doesn't happen?"

Well, they *did* begin to prepare for my replacement! But that was fine with me, because I did not want to leave them in the lurch at the last minute. I *knew* that God would not fail me!

Now, *knew* is a rather strong word! Did I ever worry, or doubt? Absolutely! But I would always refocus my thoughts back to what I knew to be true. The Word of God said that He would never fail me, so that's what I was going with!

It was the middle of July, and my home had still not sold. As a matter of fact, my realtor had assured me that my home would sell quickly, and that I would absolutely make a profit on it. She had sold multiple homes that were the exact same age and floor plan, in very similar neighborhoods, and mine was actually superior to some of those!

Yet, here we were, a mere six weeks prior to classes starting at Charis, and I had hardly even had anyone come to look at the house, let alone make an offer. Unthinkable! And I was feeling a teensy bit desperate. I wanted *out*!

Within twenty-four hours of one another, after expressing my frustration to them, both my friend Chrissy (yes, the same one!) and my mom said to me,

Derailed

"Maybe it's a heart issue!"

Um, I didn't want to hear that! But, like I said, I was feeling desperate. I was miserable at my job and was on the verge of quitting, whether I could pay my bills or not! That's not really the best attitude of faith, so with that level of desperation, I figured they were right. So, the Lord and I had a little talk.

I said, "Lord, I know You led me to go to Charis Bible College, but if there is some ungodly reason (no pun intended) that You want me to stay here, then I'll stay. I'll even have a good attitude about it (even though I don't want to)! I will! But You are going to *have* to give me the grace to do this, because I am at the end of my rope right now! I'm about to quit, regardless of whether my daughter and I end up homeless or not!"

As you can see, it wasn't the most super spiritual or faith-filled prayer! But let me tell you something: our God is faithful! Especially in those moments when we realize we absolutely cannot do what He has asked of us in our own ability, His grace is what gives us the power to do what He desires for us (Philippians 2:13).

For the next two weeks, I experienced the grace of God in a way I never had before. I'm not saying it was *easy*, but there was an *ease* to my job. People would call in sick, and somehow it didn't set me off the same way it had before. I just knew that we would find someone to fill the shift. Things that normally would get me in the worst mood still affected me, but not to the level where I took it out on others. They didn't spark my temper in the usual manner. It was a tangible change in my attitude!

Learning to rely on God's grace during that two weeks was a vital lesson I needed to learn before coming to Colorado! If we are never placed in a position that requires more of us than we are able to give in our own strength, we will never be forced to rely on the grace of God. And we must learn to stay in that position of living from His grace, His ability, at all times.

On August 9th, at eleven o'clock at night, *less than a month* before classes at Charis began, I received an offer on my home! Even though it wouldn't close until the end of September, I thought, *We're outta here!*

Of course, we couldn't leave right then: there was much to do! It was a couple of weeks before leaving when I began to experience some doubt and fear. This is something that I really want to convey to you in my story: you do *not* have to be in perfect faith, all the time, every single minute of the day, for God to come through for you! However, in the midst of my uncertainty, He came through for me with another word directly from Him— and He used Daniel Amstutz and Carlie Terradez (yet again) to do it!

One day I was off from work and was feeling a bit overwhelmed and afraid. I thought, *Is this really what God is leading me to do right now? It's been ten years!*

Am I absolutely certain that this is God, and not just my desire to get away from where I am? There was a distinct possibility that I had just come up with this idea on my own as a way to escape the difficulties I was facing. I had done that before: when things got tough, I ran away! Was I doing the same thing this time?

I spoke to Chrissy again—poor thing! I think back, and man, she dealt with a lot of whining from me over the years! At any rate, she agreed that, yes, I needed to *know* that this was God! So, I told my daughter's dad that I needed to run to town and do some errands: truthfully, I just needed some time alone to pray.

It was Thursday August 11th, 2016, and it was smack dab in the middle of the *Healing is Here* conference at the Charis Bible College campus in Woodland Park, CO. You wouldn't think that listening to a conference on my telephone would help me to accomplish my goal of "praying," but it was perfect timing!

Daniel and Carlie do absolutely wonderful workshops at these healing conferences. Carlie also assisted Daniel in founding the Healing School services that take place weekly at the college campus.

They both have a passion and gift to teach people to not only receive their healing, but also how to minister healing to others. So, as I turned on the *Healing is Here* live-stream feed, the two of them were in the middle of ministering in the sixth of these sessions.

As I began to listen, driving through town, they were talking about the story of Jesus and the disciples getting into the boat to go to the other side of the Sea of Galilee (Mark 4). Now, the disciples could probably tell there was a storm coming, but Jesus said, "Hey, guys, let's go to the other side!" So, they got into the boat.

Sure enough, in the middle of the night, a terrible storm that had been brewing came into full force! The Bible says that the wind was blowing, the waves were crashing over the sides of the boat, and it was filling up with water. The disciples were *freaking out*! Based on what it looked like and what it felt like, that boat was going down!

So, where was Jesus? He was *asleep on a pillow*! Now, those boats didn't have a compartment underneath, where Jesus was protected from the weather. He was in the exact same storm with them! It was a rough ride, and He was probably cold, and getting wet, but He was tired, so He was asleep! The disciples just didn't understand how He could do that. In fact, they woke Him up and said, "Jesus! Don't you *care* that we're all gonna die?!"

What was the difference between Jesus and the disciples? They were all in the same boat—literally! So, how could He sleep, when in the same boat, the same storm, and the same circumstances the disciples were in total fear? The difference is that Jesus *knew* that the Father had told Him to go to the other side. He also *knew* that the Father loved Him. Apparently, the disciples didn't have that same knowledge or certainty, because when they woke Him up, they even questioned His love for them!

Jesus had complete confidence in the Father—His Word and His love—therefore, He had *zero doubt* that they would safely reach the other side. It didn't matter *what* the storm looked like or felt like, or how comfortable or uncomfortable the trip was. **To Jesus, the storm was completely irrelevant!**

As Daniel and Carlie talked about this story, I heard the Lord say, "I told you, Tiffany: We *are* going to the other side... of the country!" So, I chuckled, and nodded my head. *Yes, Lord, let's go to the other side!* I may have been feeling some doubt and uncertainty, but *Jesus was in my boat!* So, my worry began to subside, and I realized that if Jesus was in my boat (and He always is) then I didn't have *anything* to worry about!

A little later on, they began to teach on watching what we speak. Without going really deeply into this teaching, I'll just say that our words, the way we speak, can influence our circumstances! So, they were talking about how important it is to speak words of faith, and not negative words of doubt and unbelief.

Now, in the past, every single time I'd heard a sermon on taming the tongue, or speaking faith, or basically just having a positive confession about things,

I'd always felt incredibly condemned! I would think, *Oh, man, I really do need to watch what I'm saying!* I mean, I'm not one who is very talented in holding back my words!

But this time it was different. I heard the Lord ask me kindly, "Tiffany... what have *you* been saying for the past six months?"

Oh, man, when He asked me that question, I began to weep in earnest, because all of those words began to pour through my mind. I'd been saying for months:

"I'm moving to Colorado to attend Charis Bible College. God is going to get us there. He's going to work everything out. It's gonna be *last minute*. It's going to be such an amazing miracle, there will be *no doubt* in anyone's mind that it was God!"

I had even forgotten that I had said that we would leave, and my house would sell at the last minute! (I mean, who in their right mind would confess *that* nonsense?!) But everything that I had been saying for six months was coming to pass exactly the way I had said it. Thank God for His wisdom and grace taking over so I did *not* submit to the world's wisdom—which is usually, "keep your mouth shut, just in case"—and instead spoke out what I believed!

Those two very simple words from the Lord to me were exactly what I needed to hear to have the confidence to *know* that, yes, it was time to go!

Derailed

God did so many amazing things to orchestrate blessings for me as we prepared to leave. First of all, I had tentatively told my employers that I would leave on August 23rd. Before my demotion in January 2016, as a district manager, I would travel from restaurant to restaurant, covering the manager's days off. The "deal" that we had made was that, although they would "check in" a new manager two weeks prior to that, I would be able to stay in my single restaurant to help her, rather than moving from store to store.

However, a few days after I received the offer on my home, my bosses informed me that the last couple weeks of my employment would be spent hopping around the different restaurants. Now, this took a lot more time than being in my own restaurant, and with all the packing and preparation that needed to be done, I didn't feel good about that. So, I politely declined, and since they were the ones who had gone back on their promise to allow me to stay put, they allowed me to resign my position early without feeling like I was abandoning them!

Then, the day that I signed my resignation paperwork, I was telling my boss that I was happy that it worked out the way it had, because I had so much to do before moving.

His boss overheard me say that, and she said, "Oh, so it was better for you? I was afraid we had really messed things up!"

I told her not to be concerned, that everything was good, and I was happy I was leaving on such good terms. In fact, I was relieved that I would have time to pack. She then proceeded to *postdate my resignation* so that I was **paid for an additional week of my salary that I didn't work**! That is the favor of God!

Around August 15th, I was scheduled to have a phone interview with the phone center at Andrew Wommack Ministries. When I had applied, they had told me that the normal shifts would be 4:30am before school and then a few hours after classes as well. My mom wondered how I could do that, as there wouldn't be anyone who would be available to babysit my daughter at 3:30 in the morning!

I told her, "If God wants me to work at the phone center, then He will work it out! If not, then He will provide an even better job opportunity for me. Either way, it'll be fine!" I had complete peace.

On the day of my phone interview, I was making deliveries of some items I was giving to different people at my restaurants, and in one of the parking lots I lost my iPhone! (I *think* it was the parking lot, I'm honestly not sure.) But the ministry was going to be calling me **within the hour** for my interview: What if I didn't answer?!

Now, I don't know about you, but my entire *life* is on my phone! I use it for everything, from texting to bill

Derailed

paying. So, this was the perfect opportunity for me to freak out! However, instead of abject panic, the Holy Spirit rose up inside of me with *complete peace*, and I began to laugh.

Identifying that the enemy was trying to distract me, to get me to take my eyes off Jesus, and open myself to defeat, I laughed at his puny attempt! Who was he to defy the plan of the Living God for my life?

After looking for a while, I gave up. I had tried to use the "Find iPhone" app on my iPad to see if I could track it using GPS, but there was no signal. (It never did turn up. It must have gotten run over or something.)

So, on to Plan B! I used my iPad to message my mom, asking her to please meet me at my home so I could use her telephone. Then, I emailed the ministry to have them call me on her phone instead of mine, rushed to my house, and waited.

Sure enough, they called me, on time, on my mom's cell. The interview went well, and they scheduled me for a group interview on August 25th. This was yet another way the Lord came through for me: not *just* in arranging the interview despite the inopportune loss of my phone, but He provided the *grace* (ability, power) to respond in *faith* when the enemy attacked.

I didn't have to try to dig deep inside of myself to pull faith out to use it effectively: I had been trusting in

God throughout the entire process, albeit somewhat imperfectly.

When you trust in the Lord, and you've planted the Word of God in your heart, the Holy Spirit will rise up on the inside of you in that time of being pressed. The Word says He will bring to your remembrance everything that you have been taught. So, you don't ever need to worry, even when you question your own ability to believe—just trust Him!

Colorado, here we come!

Chapter 8

Back on Track

NEWSFLASH: Getting back on the right track doesn't always automatically mean perfectly smooth sailing! But it's better to run *toward* God than *away* from Him.

On August 19th, 2016, I was loaded up and ready to go. My two-and-a-half-year-old daughter and I bid farewell to her daddy and drove off into our next great adventure!

I will admit, there were definitely tears on my part. It wasn't easy to leave her dad behind. There was a lot of history, a lot of time—some good, some not as good—and it was both a little scary and a little sad to move on. Yet, I knew the path ahead held an exciting future for us!

The journey from Lake City to Colorado Springs was a twenty-four-hour drive, but it took us four days. The first night we met some friends in Mississippi and stayed in a hotel. But the other three nights we were blessed to stay with very good friends. The first was the home of Jamie and Amy, the friends I had lived with in Texas for three months after leaving Charis in 2007. The second was Kevin and Chrissy, and their two boys.

I had alienated both of these close friends, hurting them during my time of rebellion against the Lord, and I had reached out to both of them within the past few years to apologize and try to rebuild the bridges I had burned. They had both graciously accepted my apology, and slowly we had been restored, although never *exactly* the way it was. Which, I don't think is necessarily due to the harm done, but simply because life goes on!

Yet, in both visits, I felt a deeper healing take place, simply through spending time with them in the flesh. In His mercy, God restored my relationships with both of these beautiful friends! I honestly don't know how they felt, but to me it felt like no time had passed at all! Isn't it fascinating that *these two* relationships were ones that were specifically fully restored on my journey *back* to Colorado, even as they had been hurt on my way *out*? It was a huge blessing: God is so good!

My daughter and I drove into Colorado Springs on August 24th. I had a studio apartment, above a garage, that was being sublet to us for a few weeks while I searched for another place to live. My mom's home had yet to sell, but I was looking for a place for the three of us.

Meanwhile, my roommate from 10 years prior, Deanna, was living in the basement of a lovely couple who rented out their three basement bedrooms to single women. By the time my sublet arrangement had ended, there was still a week of construction left to be done on the townhome I had found for us. It *just so happened* that one of those bedrooms was empty during the week we needed a place to stay!

So, did everything go perfectly smoothly? Of course not. In fact, we should actually expect things to come up, especially when we are following after God because the enemy hates it so much! There are always going to be challenges in life that pop up along the way, but God has already arranged the provision for us, before we ever had the need.

On August 25th, I had my group interview for working at the phone center, as well as registration for school. Our group interview went very well, although I think we were all a bit nervous! That was the day I first met a group of people who would remain some of my dearest friends over the following two years at Charis, and I'm sure for the rest of my life. Morgan, Ryan, Jeremy, and Pascal: **I love you all so much!**

Derailed

Surprise, surprise: I got the job! We were told that the first two or three weeks would be training, which meant an *evening* schedule. My mom was scheduled to arrive on September the 23rd. This meant that until she arrived, my work schedule would be in the *evening*, not at 4:30am! It would be no trouble for me to drop my daughter off at daycare before classes in the mornings.

In fact, I didn't begin my 4:30am shift until the day before my mom arrived, so the baby had to spend only one night with my friend Deanna, who simply took her to the daycare where she worked. From that time on, my mom was there and able to watch my daughter every day!

However, before classes began, and Mom arrived in town, things hit a bit of a snag. I had *thought* that the daycare I had found closed at 6:30pm. This meant that Deanna, who left a separate daycare job at 6pm, would have time to pick her up, and keep her until I came home from work.

I found out on Friday, September 2, the weekend before classes started, that my daycare actually closed at 6pm! This meant that I had no one who would be able to pick her up at closing time, and I would be fined (a lot) if we had to wait for Deanna to arrive. She was really the only person I knew, so I didn't have any idea who would be available to pick my daughter up in the evenings. Monday was the Labor Day holiday, so a long weekend was looming, with *no time* to make alternate daycare arrangements.

That day, my friends Chrissy and Kevin drove into Colorado Springs with their boys to visit. They were hosting a picnic for all their old friends that night, and of course we went. We had a great time, *and* a friend of theirs volunteered to come to the daycare each evening during my training and sit with my daughter until Deanna came to pick her up!

As I had expected and told my mom, God wanted me to work at AWM and **He worked out every detail!**

Driving onto the Woodland Park campus for the first time, after years of being a Foundation Builders partner and yearning to get back to the place I knew God had originally called me, I was overwhelmed!

Was I really there? It was absolutely gorgeous, and totally surreal. Even to this day, I still feel the same sense of awe at the faithfulness of God!

Do you remember when I attended the GTS in Orlando, February 2016? That I had told Andrew that I would work for his ministry one day, and Carlie Terradez told me that I was being double minded? That at that time, it seemed *impossible* that we could successfully move to Colorado for me to attend Charis?

Well, a mere **seven months later**, on September 6th, 2016, not only was I attending my first day *back* at Charis Bible College—the very thing I had yearned for with all my heart practically since the day I left—but I began orientation for my very first day as an **employee with Andrew Wommack Ministries!**

I remember that first day of school. Surrounded by hundreds of other students like me who desired to know God more and discover their destinies, it was easy for a moment to feel small and unimportant. Who was I among so many others? Yet, on day one, God set up a divine appointment to remind me how precious I am to Him.

In between class sessions, most of time, the instructors, and even many of the guest speakers, were available to shake hands and answer questions. At one point that day, during a break, I looked to the front of the room and saw Andrew and Carlie casually chatting to one another with **no one else around them!**

Now, if you aren't familiar with Charis, this may not seem unusual. However, anyone who has ever been a student, or attended either of their meetings, can tell you that there is *always a line of people* who want to speak to them! I had never seen them chatting together like that before, especially with no one else around. Honestly, I've never seen it since.

But, I thought, *Hey, two birds with one stone!* I wanted both of them to hear my testimony from our meeting in Orlando seven months before.

So, I walked up to them and introduced myself. Addressing Andrew at first, I said, "I'm not sure if you remember me, but at the Orlando GTS, I told you in the Partner Reception that one day I would work for your ministry."

Andrew slowly nodded his head and drawled, "I remember that." Now, I'd met Andrew multiple times before, had attended school (when there were maybe 80 people in our class), had sat in on his television program, etc., and (with good reason) he had never remembered me, so to me that seemed like a miracle!

Then, I reminded Carlie that I'd asked her to pray with me, and she said, "Yes, I remember! I asked you, 'What do you want?'"

I was overjoyed to tell them that not only was it my first day back at Charis Bible College after ten years, but I was also beginning orientation later that afternoon as an employee in Communication Services!

I felt so overwhelmed by the love of God, that He would have set this up for me to share my testimony with the two of them. I understand it may seem like a tiny thing to many of you, but to me it was a gigantic act of love!

Carlie then told me to share my story because people needed to hear it. The funny thing is, at that point, she only knew the part of my testimony regarding my working for the ministry. Isn't it so much more? Yet, I promised her I would, and now I've even written a book!

Derailed

This story is why I was overcome with emotion during the talent show at the end of my successfully completed first year at Charis Bible College. God had done an incredibly redemptive work in my life! He took me from complete failure to faith and victory, from a life derailed, to back on track as though my journey with Him was just beginning!

At our promotion breakfast—the equivalent of a first-year graduation ceremony—the Charis staff had named my graduating Class of 2018 "The Class of Great Exploits." At that announcement, I couldn't keep tears from streaming down my face! (Have you noticed a pattern here? I cry easily.) What an amazing blessing to have that spoken over us! I was so excited to be included in having that prophetically declared over my life.

I could go on and on and on about all of the incredible revelations, divine appointments, promotions, answered prayers, and healings that took place during my first two years as a student at Charis Bible College. I have grown so much! But this book is just my story of His redeeming love in restoring my life after my rebellion. However, there is one last, absolutely stunning step of this journey that I need to share with you that is just the icing on the cake!

To set the stage, you should know that The Barn is where we held classes at that time (By the time this book is published, we will have moved into the new Auditorium, and, it's not an *actual* barn, it's a gorgeous building!), and was the first building constructed on the property in Woodland Park that Andrew named The Sanctuary. Plaques have been hung along one hallway of The Barn, each bearing a picture of a Charis Bible College graduating class.

So, on March 12, 2018—nearly a year after our promotion breakfast, when my class was dubbed "The Class of Great Exploits"—I shared with someone the very short version of my story. I told her how I had attended Charis for the first time in 2006, but got rebellious, carnal, frustrated, and angry and hadn't finished my first year. But I continued that God is faithful, and He got me back on track!

In retelling my story that day, it made me consider where I would have been had I not rebelled back in 2007. Even though I had looked before when I first arrived, I went again to look at the plaques. I was particularly interested to see the Class of 2008, with whom I *would have* graduated had I not run away.

Back then, the classes weren't "named," like they are now. However, most of them did adopt a class scripture. But first, I simply scanned the faces, some which were familiar, and some I didn't remember at all. I looked down at Andrew, with the rest of the staff, and I thought, *Ten years later and Andrew hasn't changed a bit! Does the man not age?!* It's so interesting to me that it took so long for me to look down!

Derailed

After a few minutes of reminiscing, and marveling at how far I had come—two months shy of my upcoming graduation—I let my eyes drop to the inscription toward the bottom, at the scripture that was chosen by the Class of 2008:

> "...but the people who know their God shall be strong, and carry out **great exploits**" (emphasis mine).
> – Daniel 11:32

I staggered backward in shock, placing my hand over my mouth stifling an, "Oh my God!" The class of 2008 hadn't been named "The Class of Great Exploits," but they had chosen that scripture to represent who they were! I actually was nearly sobbing, tears pouring from my eyes, as I heard the Lord say so clearly, "I told you, Tiffany: *I never change my mind*."

God is *faithful*, even when we are not! He is not surprised when things go wrong, when the enemy comes against us, or even when we sabotage ourselves. When we take a wrong turn in life, He does not fall off of His throne, hands cradling His head, crying, "Oh My*self*, what am I gonna do about this one, now?! She's ruined everything!"

No! He doesn't react that way at all. He just calmly says, "Rerouting. Recalculating," and gets us right back on track. He simply provides a new answer for the current obstacle! When we realize this, we will *always* be able to face any challenge with joy. We recognize that what we are facing is simply an *opportunity* for God to show up!

I love this, because the Lord has taught me over the past couple of years that when something comes up, and we don't know the answer, we can say confidently, "God, I don't know *how* You're gonna pull this one off, but I can't wait to see it, because I know You *will* and it's gonna be *amazing*!"

Our God takes your test and turns it into a testimony; He will take your mess and transform it into a message! These are not simply cliché phrases: they are the truth of the nearly-too-good-to-be-true-news of the Gospel of Jesus Christ!

Are you ready to trust Him in the adventure that He has for **you**?

Chapter 9

Redemption

NEWSFLASH: This is the story of redemption, and of a God who has such a deep love for us all that our human minds cannot possibly understand its full dimensions.

Do you remember the story of the lost sheep, where the shepherd leaves the 99 to chase after the 1, or of the prodigal son returning after squandering the inheritance left to him by his father? (Read Luke 15 to reacquaint yourself.) We often consider these as stories that apply to unbelievers. We categorize redemption and reconciliation as being applicable only to those who have never known

God, who have never chosen to believe and receive what Jesus did by dying on the cross for our sin.

However, what I have come to discover is that these stories are **much more applicable to believers**: to Christians who have known the Lord and fallen away. After all, wasn't the lost sheep already a part of the flock? Wasn't the prodigal son already a member of his father's family: an heir? Unbelievers are *not* part of the flock. Unbelievers are *not* sons; they aren't even part of the Father's household!

When a sheep wanders away from the flock, she has rejected the plan of her Shepherd and taken things into her own hands (or hooves, I suppose). She thinks her own way is best, and the farther afield she strays, it becomes more and more difficult to hear the voice of her Shepherd calling, let alone follow Him back home. Yet, all is not lost! The Shepherd sets out to pursue that lost lamb. He has been given responsibility for those sheep by His Father, and He loves them, and He is determined that none of them will be plucked out of His hand!

Perhaps as the lost sheep travels farther away from the comfort and safety of the sheepfold, exposing herself to various perils and attacks, she realizes how unfamiliar the territory around her has become. Maybe there is a moment when she realizes she is alone, and yearns to return to her Shepherd, but isn't certain which way to turn. How will she find her way home? I can imagine that lost one halting in her movement away.

Perhaps, just as we are told by our parents to stay in one spot when lost, and wait for them to find us, the sheep also acquires that wisdom. She may not know the way to return, but she is hopeful that the Shepherd who loves her will come to find her and bring her home.

As the Shepherd gains ground on the sheep that has gone astray to her own way, He calls out to her. The lost sheep still recognizes her Shepherd's voice as He comes closer and closer. The sheep takes one hesitant step toward the faint calling. Then another.

The Voice calling her becomes more and more clear, and she increases her pace. Soon, she hears not only the Shepherd's voice, but the sound of His footsteps! Then the Shepherd sees the lost sheep, and she is grateful to be found! The Shepherd gathers His precious one into His arms, slings her over His strong shoulders, and swiftly carries her back into the fold. The journey takes a fraction of the time that it took the sheep to become so thoroughly lost in the first place: after all, the Shepherd knows the shortcut and straight path home!

The prodigal son was an heir: he had a rightful claim to his inheritance. I find it quite rude that he asked his father for his share before his father had even died, however, that's how the story goes! He gathered his riches, bid his father farewell, and took off. We know that the young man squandered his inheritance in riotous living, wasteful spending, and sin. Yet soon he found himself penniless: a Jewish boy, feeding unclean pigs and so hungry that he yearned for any food at all, even the slop he was serving!

An unbeliever doesn't have an inheritance to squander! Yet, as believers, that is what we tend to do with the grace of God. He has offered us an inheritance so rich, so full of blessing and favor, yet rather than prompting us to marvel at the undeserved favor He has granted to us, we abuse it. We waste it on our own plans, doing things our own way, pursuing our own lustful desires, thinking we've got it made!

Yet even though we truly are the righteousness of God in Christ Jesus, our riotous, wasteful, foolish living opens us up to poverty—not only financially, but poverty of the soul. We find ourselves all alone, without meaningful relationships, having pushed away all the family we have in Christ, open to every attack of the enemy. We have forsaken the protection of our Father's House! It is inevitable that the enemy, who as a roaring lion roams about seeking whom he may devour, pounces on us to bring devastation (1 Peter 5:8).

Yet, I had a moment just like he did, where he *"came to himself."* The action of the prodigal son returning home is not the important part of the story! Our decisions and behaviors are important, yet it really is how we respond to the prompting of the Lord that determines the outcome: good or bad. One of the most important parts of this story is that it was the Holy Spirit who brought a moment of clarity to his mind, where he could look at his situation and realize how insane it was for him to be there! "What am I doing? I could at least go back to my father, live as a servant, and get three square meals and a roof over my head!"

When a believer has run away from his Father, there is always a point where the Holy Spirit brings clarity and allows him to see his situation the way it truly is. And at that moment, there is the realization that the Father's House is way more attractive than the world! Why scrape and scrounge when the Father has provision and safety? When He provides more than enough?

So, the prodigal returned home, in shame, expecting his father to angrily berate him, to accuse, to express his disappointment in his failure. On the contrary, what he found was a father who had been watching and waiting and had seen him coming from a long way off, running to him in joy to welcome his lost son home! And not to welcome him back as a mere servant, but as a son. He put a new robe on him, a ring on his finger, sandals on his feet, and declared, "Light up the barbecue! We're having a party!!"

I wondered at this. I mean, Dad gave his son half of the inheritance already! Where did these new riches come from? Well, is there any limit to the provision of our Father? Is there only so much that He has to provide to us? Our spiritual inheritance does not have a low balance warning: it cannot be spent; it cannot be lost; it cannot be taken away! Our Father's resources are

LIMITLESS! There is no such thing as "half" in the Kingdom of God. It is always, and only, more than enough.

> *"And God is able to make **all** grace abound toward you, that you, **always** having **all** sufficiency in **all** things, may have an abundance for **every** good work" (emphasis mine).*
> *– 2 Corinthians 9:8*

All sufficiency in all things to every good work? For all who believe? That, my friends, is the limitless inheritance that we have as children of God through faith in Jesus Christ!

And this is the unending patience the Father has for us! Jesus will always come looking for His lost lambs, and the Father is always waiting for His lost sons to return home. It doesn't matter how much time has passed, how long you have been in rebellion or astray, how sunken into quicksand you have become—His hand is reaching out for you! He is still calling your name and still looking out into the distance, waiting for your return.

If anything, stop running! Just stay put, and He will find you. You already know the sound of His voice, so don't think you can't recognize it. You will follow it! Trust Him to do the heavy lifting, and know that He will always welcome you home, no matter how much you

Redemption

have done or lost. It is **NEVER** too late! He will simply accelerate the process and redeem the time.

Allow God to take your test, your mess, and your mistakes and turn them around into an amazing testimony for His glory! He did it for *this* lamb:

He will do it for you!

Chapter 10

What's Next?

I wonder if some of you are reading this and thinking, *Okay, Tiffany. God is faithful, God is good, God loves me, God will get my life back on track. I believe you! But how? What do I do now? What happens next?*

Here's the thing: There were many times during the telling of my story where I wanted to stop and show you *how* to keep yourself on track, rather than getting—or staying—derailed! Unfortunately, this book did not provide me with the opportunity to do so, because I really wanted to focus on this specific portion of my testimony. However, returning to Charis after ten years was only the beginning of the story!

I began to receive so much revelation from the Holy Spirit, so quickly, that at one point I cried out, "Stop! I can't process all of this!" Do you know how the Lord responded?

He said, "We have ten years of lost time to make up for!"

Have you made some poor decisions? Have you gone off the rails? Have you been in this place of being stuck—off track, unable to move forward—for years?

Well, not only is it **not too late** for you to get life back on track, **God will make up for all of the lost time!** He will ensure that what the enemy has stolen—even time, personal growth, revelation, and relationships—will be restored!

In my introduction I alluded to the foundational lesson that I have learned: We cannot live this victorious Christian life in our own strength, from our own efforts. The truth is, the biggest enemy we face in living victorious Christian lives is ourselves. So, in order to live the life He designed for us, we have to get out of our flesh, and let the Lord Jesus do the living through us.

The good news is that the Holy Spirit has taught me how to do that! Now, I've not attained perfection just yet,

What's Next?

but I'm certainly on the right track! So, I want to share many more testimonies and revelations that I have received with all of you. If you want to know *how* to move into that rest and freedom, allowing the Lord to have access into every single part of your life, then I encourage you to get my next book:

Child of God: Chill Out!

I will walk you through how you can *change* and move from feeling like a total failure to a champion child of the Most High God! We will discover insights into areas such as emotional healing, physical healing, financial increase, prayer, hearing God's voice, and many more!

You've read a good portion of *my story*. So, what **is** next for you?

Now it's time to start writing **your** story!

Child of God: Chill Out!

Coming Soon

Visit the *Derailed* Facebook page
for updates and information!

https://www.facebook.com/DerailedBook

About the Author

Tiffany Naiman is a 2003 graduate of Oral Roberts University, with a BA in International Relations. After graduating from Charis Bible College in 2018, she followed her passion to help others tell their stories with excellence by launching Yattira Editing Services, which has now bloomed into a full-service self-publishing company. Her heart is to share the love and power of God with everyone she can reach around the world, and to help others do the same, with excellence.

Tiffany Naiman
Yattira Editing Services
& Yattira Publishing
YattiraLLC@gmail.com

www.ingramcontent.com/pod-product-compliance
Lightning Source LLC
Chambersburg PA
CBHW071310060426
42444CB00034B/1756